SKETCHES OF OLD CAPE COD

Text by Marion Rawson Vuilleumier

Illustrations by Louis Edward Vuilleumier

The Butterworth Company
23 Traders Lane
West Yarmouth, Massachusetts 02673

Cover Sketch — Old Mill
Brewster
see Page 30

Foreword

It is hard to imagine any resort area with more attractions per square mile than Cape Cod. The visitor can immerse himself in history or folk lore, enjoy the beauties of four seasons, see present and past reminders of famous people, browse in fascinating shops - from art to antique — and frolic on surf and sand.

Many places are hidden away from speedy turnpikes and congested shopping areas. Sometimes they are missed. Here are ninety chosen from the many possibilities. With this book in hand, one can travel around the Cape, learning unsuspected facts and finding delightful surprises.

Marion Rawson Vuilleumier
West Hyannisport
Massachusetts

POINTS OF INTEREST

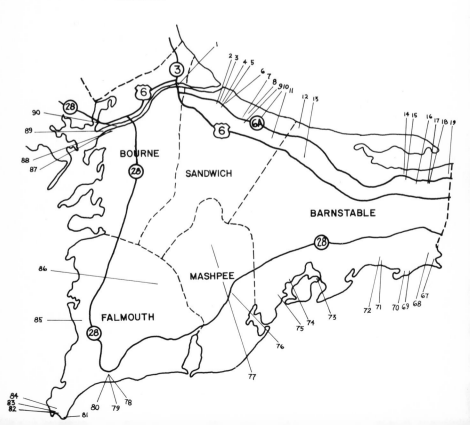

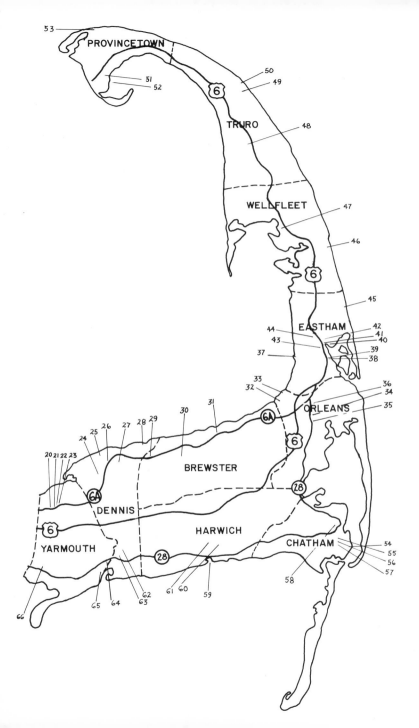

ALPHABETICAL LISTING

Page &
Map No.

SAGAMORE BRIDGE

Bourne

One gateway to the picturesque land of Cape Cod is this beautiful span which curves majestically like a rainbow over the Cape Cod Canal. From this bridge is a magnificent view of the Cape and the canal. At stopping places along the canal side one can watch tugs, tankers, freighters, fishing boats and pleasure craft use this safe passageway up the New England coast. Flags of many nations evidence the world wide use of this canal, which was opened in 1914.

This bridge was built in 1933-35. Prior to this time, travelers used an old drawbridge, one of whose abutments still may be seen farther along the canal banks. The Army Corps of Engineers maintains the canal and also has the oversight of this bridge. Its repair and maintenance is a never ending task, as it is kept safe for the thousands of tourists and residents who drive over it constantly.

1

SETH POPE HOUSE

Sandwich

In the late 1600's Seth Pope came to Sandwich to expand his business. His fleet of push carts was operating successfully in Boston and he was looking for new areas to cover. The town fathers disapproved of his ideas, considering Pope an itinerant pedlar. They sent a delegation to ask him to leave within twenty-four hours.

"I'll leave at sundown," Pope responded, "but I'll be back to buy out your town!"

Around 1700 Pope did return to Sandwich and built this lovely house on Grove Street. He also built an identical one on Tupper Road. In addition he bought and rebuilt the grist mill on the pond facing this house, giving both to his son. Pope's descendants lived here for several generations.

SANDWICH GLASS MUSEUM

Sandwich

This graceful building houses an authentic, rare Sandwich Glass collection which was made by the famous Boston and Sandwich Glass Company between the years of 1825-1888. Deming Jarves founded this industry which now has disappeared, with just a stone to mark the site. Every known type of glass was made here including blown, lacy, and pressed. Pieces were made in a great variety of colors as well as clear. They were etched, engraved, cut and painted.

Visitors from April 15 to November 15 may see such rare pieces as a ruby urn made for the Paris Centennial as well as collections of lamps, paper weights, ink wells, cup plates, candlesticks, curtain tie backs, glass knobs, plates and goblets. All were part of the 30 million dollars worth of glass produced by the Sandwich factory during its sixty-three year history.

DEXTER GRIST MILL

Sandwich

On Shawme Pond beneath graceful willows and surrounded by fluttering ducks, stands an old mill, a reminder of early Sandwich. Built by Thomas Dexter in 1654, it was the first grist mill on Cape Cod. In the beginning it housed the miller's family as well as the grinding mechanism.

Through the years the water wheel has provided power for carding and cloth-dressing, marble working, wheelwriting, tag making and printing. The mill has also served as a tea room.

Today with its earliest type of wooden machinery restored, the mill grinds corn and turns out cornmeal for the modern housewife. The location in the town's center, near the historic church, glass museum, and Hoxie House, provides a perfect showcase for an old industry.

HOXIE HOUSE

Sandwich

Though it can't be accurately documented, this house was built shortly after the town was founded in 1637. It is considered to be the oldest house on Cape Cod still standing in its original location. It is a weathered, shingled salt box with the short slanted roof in the front and the long slanted roof in the rear overlooking the quiet waters of Shawme Pond.

Rev. John Smith is reputed to have lived in this house from about 1655 to 1688. It is named, however, for Captain Abraham Hoxie, a whaling Captain who owned the house in the middle 1800's. The house was acquired by the town and restored in 1959.

Visitors may see how a Cape Cod family lived and worked in the early days, for it has been carefully furnished in the 1676-1680 period. It has many interesting features such as gun stock posts, chambered beams and wide floor boards. A small herb garden gives further atmosphere.

THE
FIRST CHURCH OF CHRIST

Sandwich

The history of this church dates back to 1637 when ten men of Saugus were granted land to settle. Shortly afterwards the Church of Christ in Sandwich was established, the first to be founded on Cape Cod.

The present church building was erected in 1847. The steeple is somewhat like that of Saint Mary-le-Bow in London which was one of Sir Christopher Wren's masterpieces. The graceful structure stands in the center of the town on a knoll overlooking the placid pond and the old mill.

Inside there are several items of great historic interest. The antique organ was built in 1847 and is notable because of its "toothpick" pedal board. The Captain Adolph bell was cast in 1675 and is believed to be the oldest church bell in America. The 1715 pulpit Bible was originally owned by one of the early ministers, Rev. Roland Cotton, and was presented to the church by his widow in 1763.

QUAKER MEETING HOUSE
Sandwich

The Sandwich Meeting of Friends was established in 1657 and is the oldest continuous Quaker congregation in America. This meeting house is the third to be built on this site and was erected in 1810. The long sheds for horses and buggies and the peaceful woodland setting give an aura of long ago which is deepened as the visitor enters the simple structure.

The plain sanctuary on the first floor is divided in half so men and women could sit separately. When completely separate business meetings were held, the central wooden partitions were lowered from the ceiling. This was done with an amazing contrivance located in the upstairs kitchen. It resembled a ship's wheel and connects with the partition by ropes and two pulleys located in the attic. The second floor also has a large dining room. When Quakers came from all over southeastern Massachusetts for Quarterly Meeting, it was a two day affair and meals were necessary.

Now the activity at the Meeting House is confined to regularly scheduled worship in July and August and to occasional other meetings for worship and business. The cemetery beside the Meeting House is still used for the burial of members and their relatives.

WING HOMESTEAD

Sandwich

This venerable home on Spring Hill Road, also known as the Old Fort House, was built by Stephen Wing in 1641. Wing was one of the town's first settlers and became the first Quaker convert when Rhode Island Quakers came to visit.

One of the two living rooms dates back to 1637, for it was a communal fort built with walls almost two feet thick to protect the settlers from the Indians. Since the Indians turned out to be friendly, the fort was not needed and Wing purchased it, incorporating it into his new home.

Wing's descendants owned the home continuously for over three hundred years and it now belongs to the Wing Family Association.

MARTHA HOXIE HOUSE
Sandwich

On a knoll at the corner of Route 6A and Quaker Meeting Road, there stands a delightful Cape Cod half house. it was originally built in 1650 on County Road in South Sandwich as a ¾ house with a bow roof. Cape three quarter houses have a window on one side of the door and two windows on the other, as against a full Cape which has two windows on each side of the door.

Cape Codders were noted for changing their houses, expanding them as families grew from half to full Capes and cutting and moving them as later family changes dictated. This house is a good example of such activity.

When Martha Hoxie owned this house at the original location, she had the structure cut in half. The side with the original door and one window was given to a friend and moved to the new location. The original door faces South, and the little house has its back turned to the busy highway. In recent years it was moved up to the knoll and an addition constructed. The remaining half with the two windows and new entrance, still stands on County Road. Measurements of both houses, including the bow roof, corroborate this history.

SKIFFE HOUSE

Sandwich

James Skiffe built this house in 1638. It was then a one story home located on Route 6A across from the Crowe Farm. In 1720 it was moved to its present location and rebuilt as a two story house. During the renovations it acquired back to back fireplaces and a space between chimneys known as the hidden room.

The imposing structure has been owned by several families including Foster, Orcutt and Bridges, with detailed records going back to 1840. It is presently under private ownership. Gustave Swift, who started the meat packing company, is reputed to have brought cattle here and butchered them for sale to workers at the Sandwich Glass Factory.

NYE HOMESTEAD
Sandwich

The Nye Homestead was built in 1685 by Benjamin Nye who came to New England much earlier on the ship Abigail in 1635. By 1643 he had reached Sandwich, for his name was on the town records as being able to bear arms. In 1669 the records show he received "twelve acres of land because he built the mill by the little pond". Later he built a fulling mill nearby. During this time he was also supervisor of highways and had a saw mill.

This house was lived in by eight successive Nye generations until 1911. A distant cousin, Ray Nye owned it awhile then presented it to the Commonwealth. In 1959 the Commonwealth of Massachusetts deeded it over to the Nye Family of America which was organized to save the historic house.

In 1936 Mrs. Helen Nye Holway at age 95 was able to recall when there had been a blacksmith shop, grist mill, carding machine, shoemaker's shop, tannery and general store all within a stone's throw of this old house. It was surrounded by forty acres of land which had abundant grape vines, fruit orchards and berry patches.

SANDY NECK

Barnstable

Driving east from Sandwich on 6A, the traveler sees beyond the shore and across a quiet cove a half mile wide strip of towering sand dunes. Called Sandy Neck, this land runs parallel to the shore for about eight miles, depending upon the amount of sand deposited or taken away from the tip by the tides. Described in 1810 by an early tourist, President Timothy Dwight of Yale, as a "long, wide fantastical beach thrown into a thousand grotesque forms by the action of wind and waves," Sandy Neck has long been a sanctuary for wild life and a fascinating spot to humans.

Indians once used the beach for oyster and clam feasts. Shifting sands occasionally expose piles of discarded shells. Later townsmen set up try-yards to convert blubber from offshore whales into oil. Then Braley Jenkins cultivated the wild cranberry bogs and ferried over pickers annually in his craft *Pomona*.

Today there is a summer colony at the end of the neck with a lonely lighthouse, beam no longer shining, standing quiet vigil. Hikers and birdwatchers who roam the dunes may see partridge, quail and ducks as they walk through the prolific holly bushes and around the old bogs where at the right time one may spot pink and purple orchids. With the balmy weather, sunbathers and picnickers arrive along with the latest sand vehicles — the beach buggies.

WEST PARISH CHURCH
Barnstable

Founded before the Pilgrims landed, the history of this church began in England in 1616. Dissenters from the Church of England met secretly, organizing the very first Congregational Church. After continuous harassments, the parish with the second minister, Rev. John Lothrop, escaped to Scituate in 1633. Then the parish moved again in 1639 to the great marshes of Barnstable.

The present structure was begun in 1717, and the first service held on Thanksgiving Day 1719. One historic feature is the golden cock weathervane atop the steeple which was sent from England. Another is the Paul Revere bell weighing 922 pounds which was cast in 1806. Stamped "Revere", it was given to the town in memory of Colonel James Otis, a native son and father of the famous patriot of the American Revolution.

Visitors should leave the main highway to see this historic church which has been completely restored. It has its entrance on the broad side, interesting box pews, great oak timbers, and a high pulpit complete with sounding board.

STURGIS LIBRARY

Barnstable

This building has the distinction of being the oldest house in America to house a library. Originally built for the Rev. John Lothrop in 1644, the house's study was used for church services until the First Parish church was completed.

This house became the Sturgis homestead when Mr. Lothrop's granddaughter Abigail married Thomas Sturgis. Here their great-great-grandson William Sturgis was born. He became one of Barnstable's famous ship captains. William went to sea at 15, becoming a master at 19. At 28 he established a Boston firm and made a fortune sending clipper ships to trade in China and the Northwest.

Just prior to his death, Sturgis purchased his old homestead which had been sold to the Chipman family. In his will he left the house to the town for library purposes. In 1867 the library was opened in one half of the house. The librarian lived in the other side. A grandson, William Sturgis Bigelow, became a library trustee and at his death in 1926, bequeathed $30,000 to the library. The money was used to establish the first stack room.

In addition to a very fine genealogical and historical collection, the library owns the original Lothrop Bible which was printed in 1603. The library also has copies of the Barnstable Patriot from 1830 to the present.

CROCKER TAVERN
Barnstable

Located on Route 6A and built in 1754, this large and comfortable Cape Cod "ordinary" fed and housed travelers during stage coach days. Coaches made regular trips from Provincetown to Plymouth and Boston, stopping here for refreshment and mail.

Cornelius Crocker owned this home for many years, then his daughter Lydia Sturgis, a widow, ran it for a long time as a public house calling it "Aunt Lydia's Tavern". These Crockers descended from John Crocker, who was the first of many Crockers to own and operate early Barnstable inns.

The center of town life, many amusing and historic events took place at this tavern. It was the headquarters for the Whigs during pre-Revolutionary days. It was also from this building one fall night in 1827 that Josiah Hinckley and Captain Joseph Bursley abruptly left their card game and raced to save important records when the countyhouse fire broke out. Unfortunately they saved only a few before the building was completely demolished.

This old hostelry is now privately owned.

COURTHOUSE CANNON
Barnstable

The cannons on the lawn of the County Courthouse once protected Barnstable residents from the British. During the War of 1812, British ships demanded of the town ransom or capture. Loring Crocker sent teams of oxen to Boston for cannons and set the big guns up on the common fields and amid the salt works. On seeing this show of arms, the British then sailed out of the harbor.

The imposing grey granite structure which looms behind the cannons, houses court sessions for Barnstable County. Completed in 1832, it succeeded one on Rendezvous Lane which was leveled by fire on October 22, 1827. In this fire many priceless records were destroyed.

The bronze courthouse bell was a gift of a widow of a foreign sea captain. When the Captain's vessel was wrecked off Sandwich, the townspeople gave him a fitting burial. In gratitude, his widow gave the German-made bell which was kept in Sandwich until 1703, then placed in the county courthouse.

OLD JAIL

Barnstable

Near the Trayser Museum on Route 6A stand the remnants of the earliest known jail of Plymouth colony, and one of the oldest wooden prison structures in New England. Constructed between 1690 and 1700, the building is typical of the 17th century architecture. It is made of heavy oak post and plank construction. On the interior walls are designs of ships and schooners as well as arrow markings scratched there by prisoners. The cell structure is small and the original locks, hinges and iron bars still remain.

The jail has been preserved through the years by being built into an old barn on Old Jail Lane. Through the efforts of the Barnstable Historical Commission, a gift of land by Mrs. Julia Chase in memory of her husband Francis, and grants of Federal and Town funds, it was possible to remove the jail to a better and more permanent place of display.

TRAYSER MUSEUM
Barnstable

This interesting brick structure on Cobbs Hill and 6A is the old Custom House. Beginning in 1789 Barnstable was headquarters of a custom district and for more than a hundred years domestic ships were registered, documented and enrolled here and foreign vessels were cleared by custom officials. Also, cargoes were bonded, bounties were paid to fishermen and other activities connected with maritime commerce took place. In 1913 this period ended when Barnstable was merged with the Boston Customs District. Then the building was turned over to the Post Office Department for handling of mail.

Finally, on February 12, 1960, the building was given to the Town of Barnstable by the Federal Government. It was then designated a museum and named for a former editor of the Barnstable Patriot Donald Trayser, Cape writer who edited the voluminous town history, *"Barnstable Three Centuries a Cape Cod Town"*. Three historical societies are in charge: Hyannis Historical Society, Historical Society of the Town of Barnstable and Tales of Cape Cod, Inc. The Cotuit Historical Society was involved for a time. Sometimes referred to as Barnstable's Memory Bank, it is open to visitors in the summer.

In this spot was buried the
SACHEM IYANOUGH
the friend and entertainer
of the Pilgrims, July 1621

erected by the Cape Cod Historical
Society

IYANOUGH'S GRAVE

Cummaquid

In 1621 when the Pilgrims came to Barnstable in search of young John Billington, who had strayed down Cape to the Nauset Indians, they were welcomed by Iyanough, Chief of the Mattakeese. According to the Pilgrim party, Iyanough was "a man very personable, gentle and courteous — about twenty-six years of age". The Chieftain, who accompanied the Pilgrims to Nauset to retrieve John, died not long afterwards in 1623.

When workmen were ploughing a Cummaquid field in 1861, they uncovered a large brass kettle. Under it was a skeleton in a sitting position. A stone pestle was on the right arm and a decayed bow and arrow on the left. A hatchet and an earthen dish were at the feet. Also in the grave were iron nails and black and white wampum. It was designated Iyanough's grave.

Tales of Cape Cod, the Capewide historical society, now owns the site, which is just off Route 6A. Walk north along a driveway by the sign and follow a stone wall east, then proceed north again to find the marker.

SALT BOX ON CAPTAINS' MILE

Yarmouthport

Between Willow Street in Yarmouthport and Union Street in Yarmouth there is a historic stretch of road on Route 6A called Captains' Mile. This beautiful example of an authentic salt box is one of many that line both sides of what is now an official historic district. Many like this are privately owned. Others, like the Bangs-Hallet House, the Colonel John Thacher House and the Winslow-Crocker House are owned by historic societies and are open for public viewing.

As many as fifty ship captains lived in Yarmouth at one time, many on this stretch of highway which was originally an Indian path and which the first settlers named the Kings Highway. Later it was known as Cranberry Highway and Route 6A. In the 1840's, Amos Otis, Oliver Hallet and Edward Thacher planted the slender saplings which grew into the enormous elm trees that line Captains' Mile. These give a cathedral effect that enchances this historic strip of earth.

WATERING TROUGH

Yarmouthport

The elaborate trough on Route 6A is a memorial to Nathanial Stone Simpkins who loved animals and nature. The charming wrought iron arch was erected in 1928 by his wife, Mabel. Pictured here are soaring ducks, a high stepping horse and a pointing spaniel. The inscription reads: "Friend of Mankind; Kind to Men's Friends". This arch is a favorite frame for photographers who wish an unusual picture of a Cape road lined with trees and old homes.

Simpkins has two other memorials. He founded two of the Cape Cod newspapers, the Barnstable Journal (Patriot) and the Yarmouth Register. These two papers have vied with each other through the years. In the administrations of Jackson and Van Buren the air crackled with sarcasm and biting inferences, delighting customers who bought both and enjoyed the battle of words.

PARNASSUS BOOK SERVICE
Yarmouthport

This fascinating book shop on Route 6A is a book lover's trap! On the outside, sheltered from the weather, is a large selection of books selling for twenty cents to one dollar. Browsers may buy day or night, dropping the money through the shop's mail slot.

On the inside, behind stacks of new and old books, the genial proprietor Ben Muse may be found with a pencil behind his ear usually discussing rare books with some ardent book worm. The shop is internationally known, for sixty percent of its business is done by catalog to colleges and universities, many overseas.

The three story frame structure was erected in 1840 and was originally a general store run by A. Knowles. The second floor was once a Swedenborgian Church until the congregation raised enough money for a separate building. A variety of shops has occupied the first story until the building was purchased by Mr. Muse.

The book shop was so named because Mt. Parnassus was the home of the Muses.

COLONEL
JOHN THACHER HOUSE

Yarmouthport

This stately house was the ancestral home of the Thachers, who were among the first settlers of Yarmouthport. Anthony and his wife arrived from England in 1635, having survived a fierce shipwreck which took their four children. After living a year in Marblehead where their son John was born, they moved to Yarmouthport. John grew up to be a dashing army officer, a terror to the Indians.

Built in 1680, this house began life on Shore Road and was later moved to its present location on 6A. At that time the left hand side was added to the original building. After being in the Thacher family for generations, it was willed to the Society for the Preservation of New England Antiquities.

Today it is open to visitors. Prominently displayed among the authentic period furnishings are a scarlet coverlet and an old oaken cradle. The former came to Yarmouthport with the original Thachers and has been used to cover many Thacher progeny including those of Captain John, who had twenty-one children.

JOSIAH DENNIS MANSE

Dennis

On the corner of Nobscusset and Whig Streets, stands a venerable patriarch of Cape Cod houses, dating back to 1736. An original two story salt box, the house is situated on three acres of land bounded by a creek and an old stone wall.

Rev. Josiah Dennis, after graduating from Harvard College, became first minister of the East Precinct of Old Yarmouth, which later became the town of Dennis. Mr. Dennis must have had a fruitful and memorable pastorate, for the town was named for him at its incorporation, fully thirty years after his death. Dennis is said to be the only town in the United States that owns a house of this age built for the man for whom the town was named.

The old manse has ten rooms and five fireplaces, one of which has a rare 18th century deep oven. Notable also are the wide boards in the panelling, wainscoting and flooring, as well as the different types of corner columns, including a "gun stock". In the house also is the rare primitive portable pulpit desk used by Mr. Dennis.

CRANBERRY BOG

Dennis

Bogs like the above are sprinkled profusely all over the Cape. Cranberries have always grown wild here, enjoyed by the cranes and the Indians, who introduced them to the Pilgrims. In 1677 colonists sent ten barrels to King Charles II.

Henry Hall of Dennis is reputed to be the originator of the modern cranberry bog. Around 1816 he discovered the prolific growth of vines set out in sandy top soil in a moist pasture. He experimented, growing larger and larger berries. By 1845 when white sugar became easily available and made the berry more palatable, the cranberry boom began.

Bogs are flooded in winter, then cultivated during the summer. Harvest time is in the early fall. Once schools on the Cape adjusted their schedule to cranberry picking time.

The little red berry is still a very important part of Cape Cod's economy.

CAPE PLAYHOUSE

Dennis

This structure began life in 1680 as the Nobscusset Meeting House. Through the years it has been rolled to various locations and has served as a school, barn, tin shop, slaughterhouse and garage. In 1927 Raymond Moore remodeled it and opened the first summer theatre on Cape Cod. It was also the third in the nation.

On its stage have played many noted stars, including Gregory Peck, Robert Montgomery, Bette Davis, Henry Fonda and the late Gertrude Lawrence. The latter's husband, Richard Aldrich, ran the playhouse for a time. Each summer the theater hosts Broadway hits and pre-Broadway shows. It still deserves its description of "Cradle of Stars".

Nearby is the Cape Cinema which is famous for its gigantic mural done by Joe Mielziner and Rockwell Kent. On the grounds also are cottages for stars, workers and sponsors as well as a scenery shop and a dining room.

SCARGO TOWER

Dennis

A massive stone tower, just off Route 6A, caps one of the highest points of land on Cape Cod. Scargo Hill rises 160 feet above sea level and has a commanding view of Cape Cod Bay from Manomet Cliffs to Provincetown. This hill served as a beacon to mariners long ago, who were inbound to such active ports as Brewster, Dennis, Yarmouth and Barnstable.

This round stone structure which rises 28 feet from the top of the hill, was erected in 1902. It was a gift of two hometown boys, Frank and Charles Tobey, who had made good in the furniture business in Chicago. The tower, the hill and the beautiful lake below were named for the legendary Princess Scargo of the Nobscussett Tribe, daughter of Sachem Sagam.

SHIVERICK SHIPYARD

East Dennis

On the shores of Sesuit Harbor stands a stone monument erected to commemorate one of the vanished Cape industries, the "backyard ship builders". In 1849 three brothers, Asa, Paul and David Shiverick, joined with Christopher Hall, a retired ship master and owner, to form the Shiverick Shipyard. During its ensuing thirteen years of existence, it produced twelve ships, all made by hand. Some say their design has never been surpassed for construction, speed and beauty.

Eight ships were clippers of 1,000 to 1,500 tonnage. Four ships were smaller schooners. The first craft launched was the *Revenue* in 1850, and there was a steady procession thereafter. The complete list is on the granite marker. Also, the marker has a map of the yard, which consisted of a dock, caulking shop, saw pit, blacksmith shop, ways, and a main work shop. A footbridge across the salt marsh connected the yard to the area of worker homes on Quivet Neck. In those days the inlet was much larger.

Three of the most famous clippers built here were the *Webbfoot*, the *Wild Hunter* and *Belle of the West*. *Wild Hunter*, with Joshua Sears at the helm in 1856, was famous for making the run from Boston to San Francisco in 108 days. The *Belle of the West* ran for some years between India and England. The *Webbfoot* in 1864 with Milton Hedge as master, made a run from Calcutta to New York in 85 days.

DILLINGHAM HOUSE

West Brewster

A gray shingled salt box on Route 6A represents one of the earliest styles of Cape Cod architecture. This is the answer skilled builders gave to the need for larger houses that still fitted the rolling landscape. This style rises two stories in front with a short slope to the ridge pole. In the back there is a long easy slant, almost to the ground. The salt box designation comes from its similarity to the top of the wooden salt boxes that once occupied important places in Cape kitchens.

The architectural patriarch was built by Quaker Isaac Dillingham in about 1659 and is believed by many to be one of the very oldest houses standing on Cape Cod. Later structural additions have somewhat changed but have not obliterated this home's earlier lovely lines.

OLD MILL
West Brewster

This excellent example of an old mill was built in 1873 by Bartlett Winslow and T.D. Sears. At first it was operated by a water wheel, then in 1880 a metal turbine was installed. This mill has been used variously as a grist mill, an overall factory, an ice cream plant and a family dwelling. Mr. Benjamin Ellis was the last miller to grind here regularly.

Purchased in 1940 by the town, it is now open to the public as a museum. The most exciting time to visit is in the spring when the herring are leaping and squirming up Stoney Brook to spawn in the mill ponds.

The history of the mill site reaches back 300 years to 1661 when an Eastham native, Governor Thomas Prence, was given permission by the colony court to buy land from the Indians to build a mill. In 1663 a water powered grist mill was built. Shortly after a fulling mill was erected. Later a woolen mill was built on the site of the fulling mill which had burned. A tannery was added in 1830. The area was then known appropriately as Factory Village.

FIRST UNITARIAN-
UNIVERSALIST SOCIETY
Brewster

Built in 1834, this church is the third erected on the site. The first was the old Meeting House built around 1700 when the town was still part of Harwich. The church was then referred to as North Precinct, Harwich. The present structure is known as the Captain's Church because of the Captains' names on the pews. There were ninety-nine ship captains who called Brewster home. This town is reputed to have had more deepwater captains in proportion to its population than any town in America.

The white spired church is also noted for its antique flags, its parish house which is historic Dawes Hall and for its ancient burying grounds. Here are memorial stones for fifty men who were lost at sea. Also in this cemetery are stones for Captain Rene Rousseau, one of the many individuals rumored to be the lost Dauphin of France, and Captain Elkanah Crosby, father of eight girls. Seven of his daughters married sea captains, the other dying in infancy.

CAPTAIN LINNELL HOUSE

Orleans

On Skaket Road stands this authentic French villa, built by a Cape Cod Sea Captain. On this same site in 1835, Captain Ebeneezer Harding Linnell had built a Cape Cod house for his bride, Rebecca Byron Crosby. Then in 1850, when Captain Linnell was waiting in Marseilles for his ship *Buena Vista* to be unloaded, he was invited by his agent to visit a new villa in the suburbs. Captain Linnell was charmed by the house and obtained the plans.

On returning to the Cape, the Captain commissioned his father-in-law Edmund Crosby to build the French villa and had it attached to the Cape Cod house. Much later he had the small Cape Codder detached and moved across the road.

Captain Linnell, who became a world famous clipper ship captain at the helm of his speedy ship the *Eagle Wing*, never retired in his lovely French villa. On what was to be his final run with the *Eagle Wing* before retiring, a vicious squall off Rio de Janeiro ended his career.

This house is now a restaurant with charming atmosphere.

ROCK HARBOR
Orleans

This peaceful harbor was the scene of a battle in the War of 1812. A British fleet under Admiral Lord Howe was sent along the coast to demand money from the various towns in return for not destroying their salt works. Two Cape towns paid the ransom. Orleans' share was $2,000 and the citizens refused to pay. Commodore Richard Ragget of the ship *Spencer* was sent to collect. His men were turned back by musket shots from the militia.

Later in December of 1814, the British frigate *Newcastle* was patrolling and went aground on the flats — to the jeers of the Orleans townsfolk watching on shore. The Captain got his vessel afloat then, in retaliation, sent a barge into Rock Harbor to capture three sloops and the schooner *Betsey*. Two sloops were burned and the third captured and sent to Provincetown. The schooner *Betsey* was also taken. The young midshipman in charge ordered her watchman, an Orleans man, to pilot her out of the harbor. The Cape Codder loyally ran the *Betsey* aground on the flats near Yarmouth and she was recaptured by the townsfolk.

Since the bounty wasn't paid, and the *Betsey* was recovered, the victory of the Battle of Rock Harbor was popularly awarded to Orleans.

JOSHUA CROSBY HOUSE

East Orleans

On Tonset Road stands this 165-year-old house which began life in classic Cape Cod style with two windows on each side of a central door. Built by Abner Freeman in 1804, it was a wedding gift to Joshua Crosby and Sarah Freeman. A growing family caused the addition on the right. By extending the house beyond the windows the lovely full cape was thrown out of proportion.

Crosby had a colorful career first as a whaler, then as a gunner on a boat that traveled shipping lanes harassed by the Barbary Coast pirates. During the War of 1812, he was gunnery officer on the *Constitution* when it captured the *Guerriere*.

Finally retiring to land, he operated for a time the trio of lights at Nauset known as the "Three Sisters". Then he became an Orleans farmer until his death in 1861.

THE CHURCH
OF THE HOLY SPIRIT
Orleans

In the summer of 1933 a tiny church seating fifty people was built and dedicated. Seventeen members were in the first congregation. Richard Kimball, a retired writer who donated the land, became the lay preacher. Others made donations to make the little church possible. A fanlight from a demolished mansion came from Beacon Hill, handmade shingles arrived from South Carolina and crucifixes were carved by a blind Italian laborer.

The parish prospered, and Mr. Kimball took courses enabling him eventually to become a minister. Mrs. Kimball established the Craft Guild and founded the Galley West Gift Shop where handcrafted articles made by parishioners are still sold.

Later several fascinating structural additions were made and the church became a year round parish. Its many hand crafted appointments and its charming Cape setting make it well worth visiting, especially on a summer Sunday.

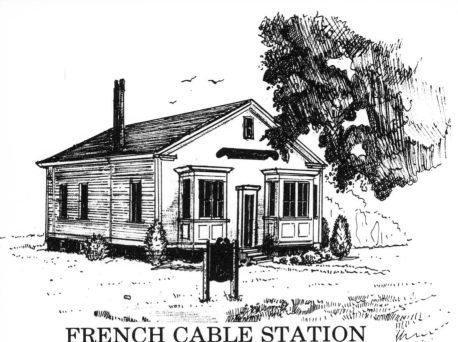

FRENCH CABLE STATION
MUSEUM
Orleans

On Route 28 near Cove Road stands a modest white frame building which houses the only cable station remaining in the United States. Built by a French Cable Company in 1890, it housed cable equipment which transmitted messages across the ocean to Brest, France. Daily stock transactions as well as news were transmitted to Europe and this was the main method of international communication from 1890-1940. The last transmission was on the eve of Thanksgiving 1959. The cable method had been made obsolete by the wireless and radio.

Fortunately no one disturbed the interior since it was the property of a French company. In 1971 the station was purchased by a group of public spirited citizens and the building is now open summers as a museum. The cottage-type exterior belies its business-like interior, for it is filled with transmitting equipment, cables, recorders and testing machines. The original gray cables, thick as a man's wrist, snake along a brick basement wall and out into the ground toward Town Cove. The Superintendent's office contains the original desk, faded records and graphics prepared by the Smithsonian Institution.

FIRST ENCOUNTER BEACH
Eastham

On this lonely shore in 1620, the Pilgrims first encountered the Indians. The Pilgrims had come from Provincetown where the *Mayflower* anchored as it arrived in the new world. While traveling this stretch of marsh and sea, the Pilgrims were greeted with Indian shouts and a shower of arrows. A few muskets were fired in return and no further trace of hostile Indians was seen.

The Nauset Indians could be excused their unfriendly welcome, for they had memories of Captain Thomas Hunt who four years earlier had kidnapped several Indians and taken them to Europe.

Eventually the Indians and Pilgrims became friends, largely through the influence of Massasoit. When the settlers came to Eastham later, the Indians gave them a more peaceful welcome.

CAPTAIN PENNIMAN HOUSE

Eastham

Captain Edward Penniman was a whaling-ship master who made a fortune at sea. He commanded several vessels including the *Eugenia*, named for his son Eugene who also became a whaling captain.

In 1876 Captain Edward Penniman retired and built the most expensive house in Eastham. This French Empire (Victorian) style structure stands on high land on Governor Prence Road. Its mansard roof, which gives a great deal of interior space in the upper story, is a distinctive feature of this elaborate home. Also noteworthy is the cupola, matching barn and whale jawbone back gateway.

The home is kept in excellent condition by the present owner, the Cape Cod National Seashore Park.

WHALEBONE GATE

Eastham

A fine example of a whale jawbone gate stands near the rear entrance of the Captain Penniman House in the Cape Cod National Seashore Park. There were many of these gates on Cape Cod when whaling was part of the Cape's economy.

Whales were plentiful off shore in the early days. Indians used to spear the whales that came near shore, then tug the carcasses to shore from their log floats and cut them up for meat. Later the settlers followed the same procedure and cut the blubber off, refining the oil in Try Yards. Off shore whales became scarce in the 18th century, and residents took to sea to hunt whales all over the world.

These graceful gates are made by burying the whale jawbones in the ground for well over a year. This allowed for natural processes to clean and whiten the bones before they were erected at entrances.

INDIAN SHARPENING ROCK

Eastham

The Nauset Tribe of the Wampanoag Indians lived in the Eastham area during and prior to the Pilgrim days. They used this rock for a community grinding stone. The broad channels were used to sharpen stone axes. The nearly flat surfaces were used to grind the cutting edges of tomahawks and chisels. The narrow grooves were used to form v-shaped bone fish hooks.

Originally the rock lay embedded on the beach at the western shore of Nauset Harbor. In recent years, officials of the Cape Cod National Seashore Park have raised the ancient stone to Skiff Hill and placed it under a protective shelter.

VISITORS CENTER
CAPE COD NATIONAL
SEASHORE PARK

Eastham

In 1961 Congress authorized the establishment of the Cape Cod National Seashore Park. The purpose was to preserve the natural beauty, wild life, historic atmosphere, towering dunes, salt marshes and great beaches of Cape Cod.

The main entrance of the park is at Eastham in this Visitor's Center which overlooks Salt Pond and the ocean. Thousands of visitors each year see the exhibits, obtain information of the area, hear the park lecturers and follow the nature trails.

The park territory also extends into the towns of Truro, Wellfleet and Provincetown.

OLD SCHOOL HOUSE

Eastham

This little one room district school house built in 1869, is now the home of the Eastham Historical Society. For seventy years this building fulfilled its initial function of housing a school. Now it is a museum, housing an extensive collection of artifacts of old Cape Cod.

Located at the entrance of the National Seashore Park's Visitor's Center, this charming bit of old Cape Cod is a popular place. Visitors may see within displays of yesteryear's tools, photographs of old Eastham, intricate and authentic scrimshaw, Indian arrowheads and artifacts, as well as a simulation of an old time school room.

OLD WINDMILL

Eastham

This venerable example of Cape Cod windmills stands opposite the Town Hall on Route 6. Though the date 1793 has been nailed into a board inside the structure, the mill is probably older. It is reputed to have been built in Plymouth about 1688, then moved across the Bay to Truro about 1788. It was moved to Eastham about 1793 and is the oldest working wind-driven mill on the Cape. Seth Knowles and John Fulcher were two of its millers.

Today the ancient mill is restored to working condition. Sail is used if there is enough wind. The creaking, handmade works illustrate a long ago once vital industry that made millers important men.

OLD CROSBY TAVERN

Eastham

On Bridge Road stands an old Cape Cod home that is believed to be 250 years old. Local historians feel it was built in 1720, though 1750 is the date over the door. It became the parsonage of the Rev. Edward Cheever when he came to Eastham in 1750. After his death it was sold to Thomas Crosby, who turned it into Crosby's Tavern and Stage Coach stop.

During the War of 1812 it served briefly as a jail for twenty-three seamen of the *H.M.S. Spencer*. The British ship had captured Captain Matthew May and pressed him into service as a navigator. The wily Cape Codder ran the ship aground enabling the militia to capture the Britishers and incarcerate them briefly in the Tavern while awaiting the trip to Boston.

Captain Joshua Nickerson bought the tavern in 1830 for a home. Since then it has been lived in by a succession of Cape Codders.

NAUSET LIGHT

Eastham

A light first shone at Nauset in 1838 when three brick towers were erected, for skippers in those days identified lights by their numbers.

Gradually the coast retreated and the towers tumbled over the cliff. Three octagonal structures made of wood replaced them in 1892 because they could be more easily moved as the cliff retreated. These lights were known as the "Three Sisters".

The present light was moved from Chatham in 1923 when that light ceased to need twin beacons. Skippers at this time began identifying lights by the number of flashes.

The nearby house is now privately owned but once was the lighthouse keeper's home until the light was made automatic several years ago.

MARCONI STATION

Wellfleet

In January 1903, Guglielmo Marconi sent the first wireless message from this location. The message was a greeting from President Theodore Roosevelt to King Edward of England. The King responded, thereby proving Marconi's long period of experimentation had resulted in success.

For fifteen years the station transmitted to an area varying from 1,600 to 3,500 miles. The term Marconigram became a household word. With the coming of World War I the station was closed by the government. The buildings fell into disrepair and crumbled away.

Today this historic spot is part of the Cape Cod National Seashore Park. An interpretive shelter and tablets commemorate its story. Inside the shelter is an exact replica of the original station. The only remnants of the actual station are some rubble and a few "deadmen" which were used to anchor the four 210-foot towers which supported the antenna.

CHAPEL OF
ST. JAMES THE FISHERMAN
Wellfleet

This unusual summer chapel, built in 1957, stands on a pine covered hill overlooking the Mid-Cape Highway. Architect Olav Hammerstrom designed a contemporary building with interior beams that remind one of the ribs of Wellfleet fishing vessels. The scallop motif, the town's emblem, repeats the sea theme, while the soaring bell tower thrusts the cross into the Cape sky for a beacon to fishermen and sailors.

The altar is in the center of the structure with the pews in a circle around it. No one is more than four seats away from the altar. Clergy, choir and lay reader seats are with their families, making participation and informality natural.

The late Bishop James Pike was influential in the chapel's beginnings while he was Dean of the Cathedral of St. John the Divine in New York City. Bishop Pike was the first summer "Priest-in-charge". The chapel has sometimes affectionately been called "Pike's Peak".

HILL OF CHURCHES

Truro

Just west of Route 6A and south of Corn Hill is the bleak "Hill of Churches," also called the "Hill of Storms". On it are two old cemeteries, sometimes referred to as "eternity acres". Here the gravestones are fascinating reading and give a glimpse of bygone years.

One marble shaft is a memorial to fifty-seven citizens of Truro who lost their lives in the great October gale of 1841. Eight of the town vessels were fishing for mackerel off Georges Banks when storm warnings rose. All headed for the Cape. One ship made port. The other seven and their fifty-seven occupants were lost. Truro lost the most of any Cape town. One of those who never returned was only eleven years old. Nine were fifteen years old and the majority of the rest were in their twenties.

On this hill is the Congregational Church built in 1827. It is known as the Bell Church because of the Paul Revere Bell in the steeple. The windows are made of Sandwich glass and the window catches are miniature iron whales.

The town building next to it was originally a church. The view from it is panoramic, especially if visitors climb to the second floor.

JENNY LIND TOWER

Truro

An unusual sight on the dunes is this old stone tower which stands on a cliff about a mile south of Highland Light. This curious structure, which is not unlike the battlements of an old Norman castle, was originally one of the towers from the old Boston and Maine Railroad Station in Boston. It was known as the Fitchburg Depot.

In 1850 when Jenny Lind the "Swedish Nightingale" came to Boston to give a concert, many more tickets were sold than seats were available. Those who were unable to get into the concert hall milled about unhappily outside. The ensuing near riot was averted when Jenny Lind climbed to the top of this nearby tower and sang to the disappointed throng.

In 1927 when the depot was razed, Harry Aldrich, Jr., a Boston attorney who summered in Truro, purchased the tower and brought it by rail to the Cape town. It was erected on its present location in memory of Harry Aldrich, Sr.

HIGHLAND LIGHT

Truro

More vessels have been lost on Peaked Hill Bars, off the 150 foot highlands of Truro than anywhere on Cape Cod. Thus in 1797 the government erected Highland (Cape Cod) Light near the clay pounds. Isaac Small, the first keeper, worked an "eclipser" which made the light a flashing beacon so it would not be confused with the Boston Light. Thoreau visited the light often, intrigued with the same problem that bothers residents today — how fast the cliff was eroding. He often descended to the beach to gaze up at the blue clay streaks in the cliff.

Rebuilt in 1857, the great tower now uses a 1000 watt electric light bulb, magnified by the great bulls eye lenses to four million candle power. This highest and most powerful of all Cape Cod lights flashes twenty miles out to sea.

PILGRIM MONUMENT

Provincetown

The 225 foot granite shaft which may be seen across the harbor, rises majestically at the Cape's tip and is dedicated to the Pilgrims. It is an eyecatching view particularly at night, when the slender shaft is floodlit and can be seen for miles. It is reputed to be the tallest masonry tower in America. The view from the top is magnificent. On a clear day the Myles Standish Monument near Duxbury may be seen, as well as the dramatic curve of the Cape and a large area of the Atlantic.

Money for the monument was raised by individuals and societies. Sums were also contributed by the town, the state and Congress. It was eighteen years in planning and is designed like one in Siena, Italy. President Theodore Roosevelt laid the cornerstone in 1907. He arrived in the presidential yacht which was appropriately named the *Mayflower,* and was accompanied by a thousand sailors and marines. Seven battleships shook the town with salutes and decorated the sky with their searchlights. The Monument was dedicated in 1910 by President William Howard Taft and Harvard's President Emeritus Charles Eliot.

At the foot of the Monument is a bas relief of the signing of the Mayflower Compact which took place in Provincetown Harbor. The Pilgrims arrived in the harbor November 21, 1620 and made preliminary explorations here before going on to Plymouth to settle permanently.

THE HARBOR

Provincetown

Just off Commercial Street in the protected harbor are the wharves by which the fishermen of Provincetown have made their living through the years. Here, the last Sunday in June, occurs the colorful pageant of the Blessing of the Fleet.

MacMillan Wharf was named for the famous native son, the late Commander Donald B. MacMillan, who went with Admiral Perry to the North Pole. Commander MacMillan and his wife made many explorations above the Arctic Circle and befriended the Eskimos, helping with their education.

A wharf here was also the scene of the first Provincetown Playhouse in 1915. George Cram Cook assembled a group of kindred spirits including Susan Gaspell and Robert Edmond Jones and they presented plays in the fish-house on the wharf owned by Mary Heaton Vorse. Featured were the plays of the then unknown playwright Eugene O'Neill. This was one of the first experimental theatre groups in the country. The Wharf Players continued the tradition in 1925. Today there are still Provincetown theatre groups carrying the drama torch.

Artists are also to be found on and around these wharves, for the art colony is one of the country's largest.

COAST GUARD STATION

Provincetown

At Race Point stands this Coast Guard Station whose crew keeps constant watch over the limitless Atlantic to aid ships in distress. Once this area was called the "Graveyard of the Atlantic" because of the dread Peaked Hill Bars. Fishing vessels still breathe easier after slipping around the "Back Shore" of the Cape into the safer haven of Cape Cod Bay.

Today this area is a mecca for the sports fishermen who surf cast, for the sun bathers who love to dive into heavy surf and for the visitors in search of unspoiled sand dunes and native growth like the bayberry.

The station is in the Province Lands which have an interesting history and for which the town is named. In 1691 this area, which was always held in common with no private ownership, was given to the Commonwealth of Massachusetts. This included the whole town. Since it was difficult for townspeople to prove ownership of their homes under this arrangement, in 1893 the state surrendered ownership of the two mile strip of shore which included the village proper. All else remained as Province Lands and eventually became part of the Cape Cod National Seashore Park.

COAST GUARD LIGHT

Chatham

This light house is part of the Coast Guard Search and Rescue Station. Originally there were two lights here but one was moved to Nauset. A light has shone from this headland since 1808. As the sea encroached, towers have toppled, so the light house is not the original structure. Its present light is 2.9 million candlepower. It gives warning of some of the most dangerous waters along the coast.

The Coast Guard Station also has radar, a weather warning system and a radio beacon. Its equipment consists of a 44-foot motor life boat, an outboard, and a Duck to meet emergencies. It is on a 24-hour a day alert and has planes, helicopters and cutters available in case of need.

Near the station is a memorial shaft to those lost on the wreck of the ship *Wadena* in 1902. Countless ships have gone down off the treacherous outer shoals of Cape Cod beginning with the first recorded one, the wreck of the *Sparrowhawk* in 1626 off Nauset. Bartholomew Gosnold recorded the peril of the shoals off Chatham, calling them "Tucker's Terror".

WINDMILL

Chatham

An old windmill was built in 1797 by Benjamin Godfrey on the hill above Mill Pond. Christopher Taylor, known affectionately as "Uncle Tap Taylor" was the succeeding owner and operator through Civil War times, when Oliver Eldridge took title. In 1874 Zenas Nickerson began milling corn, rye and wheat, continuing until 1894. George Nickerson then ran it for his own use for four years. In 1898 it was owned by Charles Hardy and was used to grind grain for exhibition only.

In recent years the mill was moved to its present site in Chase Park and given to the town by Mr. and Mrs. Stuart Crocker. Maintained by the Park Department, it is open to visitors. Corn is ground when the wind is just right. Velocity must not exceed 25 miles per hour.

Text on monument: SAMUEL DE CHAMPLAIN THE FIRST WHITE MAN ON THESE SHORES LANDED HERE OCTOBER 1606

CHAMPLAIN MONUMENT

Chatham

Just off the south end of Stage Harbor Road, stands a granite marker commemorating the arrival of one of the early explorers, Samuel Champlain. In October of 1606 Champlain landed at Stage Harbor during the course of his voyage to explore and map the Cape coastline.

During a two week stopover, he and his sailors met the Monomoyieks, the local Indian Tribe that was part of the larger Wampanoag Federation. Champlain's crew obtained fresh water, baked bread and repaired their vessel, all the while keeping a distrustful eye on the natives. Sieur de Poutrincourt, Champlain's sailing master, aggravated the Indians by firing his musket repeatedly.

Eventually a skirmish occurred and three Frenchmen as well as eight Indians were killed. Champlain immediately sailed away. This incident and a similar one that occurred at Nauset during the same voyage left an aura of distrust of white men upon the part of the Indians. This and the conduct of the infamous Captain Hunt who kidnapped several Indians, was responsible for the understandably unfriendly greetings received by the Pilgrims when they explored Provincetown in 1620.

ATWOOD HOUSE

Chatham

Captain Joseph C. Atwood built this full Cape with a gambrel roof on Stage Harbor Road in 1752. His heirs lived in it until 1926 when it became the home of the Chatham Historical Society.

Over 2,000 exhibits relating to Chatham and its people are displayed for summer visitors. The oldest article is a book of sermons published in England in 1635 that was found in the attic of the Old South Church in Boston. A salt works model, a fully equipped cobbler's bench, a relic from the *U.S.S. Constitution* and the old housing from the Chatham Light are also noteworthy.

The Joseph C. Lincoln collection is an important exhibit. In a wing added for that purpose one can see the noted Cape author's writing desk, pen and ink stand, a lifelike portrait and all of his original hand written manuscripts. Outside is a replica of an 18th century herb garden.

RAILROAD MUSEUM

Chatham

Near the end of Depot Street is the old Chatham Railroad Station, which was used by the railroad from 1887 to 1937. Railroads arrived on the Cape in 1848 when the first train chugged from Middleborough to Sandwich. By 1854 the line reached Hyannis. Extensions were made to Orleans in 1865, to Wellfleet in 1869 and Provincetown in 1873. The Chatham spur, which this station serviced, was the last built.

The gingerbread decorations on this old depot remind us of the Victorian era. After the building was no longer needed, it was given to the town by Mrs. Phyllis Cox of Chatham and Cleveland, Ohio.

The building was opened as a Railroad Museum in 1960. It contains models, documents, photographs and other memorabilia of old railroading days. The public may view this display in summer.

WYCHMERE HARBOR

Harwich

Once this lovely circle of water was a race track. A sea captain who retired after the Civil War bought a fast mare and created a half mile track for racing. When not caring for his cranberry bogs, he raced with other old timers for prizes like fifty bushels of oats. A hotel named Sea View stood on the north side and its porch made a good grand stand. Retired captains who no longer could race their ships at sea, enjoyed carrying on the tradition with their horses on land.

After several sou'easters, water broke through the dyke on the south side, which was very close to the shore. The town fathers repaired the break once, then again. Finally they decided they would rather go back to boat racing and fishing and race their horses elsewhere. A channel was cut and the pond was dredged. Now graceful boats like this fill the picturesque harbor. A cottage colony called Wychmere was begun here in the 1880's, hence the name.

SQUIRE LONG HOUSE
South Harwich

The oldest house now standing in Harwich is located just off Chatham Road and Main Street at the rear of the original Long property. It was built in 1765 by John Long who was a successful farmer. According to the town report of that year, the building was 924 square feet in area and had fourteen windows or 64 feet of glass. Houses were valued by their windows then and the worth of this house was listed as $500.00. A porch was a later addition in 1789.

John Long's youngest son James lived here for many years and was known as the "Squire". He was quite prosperous and was at various times a Selectman and a Justice of the Peace. For eleven years he served as a member of the legislature.

BROOKS ACADEMY

Harwich Center

This lovely white edifice with the graceful columns was erected in 1844 by Sidney Brooks. Known as the Pine Grove Academy, it housed the first maritime school in the country. Here Cape students learned the art of navigation in preparation for their coastal and world wide voyages.

The building was given to the town by Mr. Brooks and now houses the Harwich Historical Society. Here items of particular interest to the town are on display Monday, Wednesday and Friday afternoons during the summer months. A wing added later houses offices.

Nearby is an old Powder House used from 1770 to 1864.

CONGREGATIONAL CHURCH

South Dennis

Just off Route 28 on Route 134 stands an old white church which is full of unique objects. The organ is the oldest, dating back to 1762. It was built in London by John Snetzler and acquired by this church in 1854. Snetzler was the organ builder who made one for Handel, so visitors to this church can see an organ built by a master and lovingly restored.

The 10 by 6 foot mural *Adoration* by Edwin Howland Blashfield is much prized. In addition this church has a chandelier of Sandwich glass dating from 1835. The clock and the bell are also noteworthy.

The church is more than a museum, however. It has a very active congregation and is busy every day with all age groups — from pre-school to golden age. It sits on a knoll flanked by an ancient graveyard, still very much a village center, like the many other churches of all faiths on Cape Cod.

JERICHO HOUSE

West Dennis

Built in 1801 for Theophilus Baker, stage coach passengers passed the doorway of this house. Owned by Bakers for several generations, it is in the area formerly called Bakerstown, just off Route 28 at Trotting Park Road. This story and a half Cape with its slightly bowed roof is typical of the area.

Elizabeth Reynard, a Cape author, purchased the house and began restoration, for it had been sadly neglected. She called it Jericho for the "walls were tumbling down". At her death the house was left to her cousin Dr. Virginia Gildersleeve, Dean Emeritus of Barnard College, who gave it to the town in 1962. She stipulated that the name Jericho be kept.

The town completed restoration and set up several fascinating exhibits. Summer visitors may see here in the barn museum a typical country store corner and a display on the cranberry industry which began in Dennis in 1816.

QUAKER MEETING HOUSE

South Yarmouth

Once so many residents of South Yarmouth belonged to this Friends Meeting that the town was called Quaker Village. The first Quakers came to the Cape from England and their visits resulted in permanent meetings in Sandwich and Yarmouth. The latter dates from 1659 when the first Friend moved here from Sandwich. At first, meetings were held by him weekly alone until neighbors joined in. Then a meeting house was erected on Follin's Pond, farther up the Bass River than this present one. A sign and visible boundaries of the burying ground still mark the first site.

This present meeting house dates from 1809. It is consistent with the Quaker belief in simplicity. There is a partition to divide the sexes when separate business meetings were held. Outside there is a burial ground where markers are of uniform size and there are no epitaphs. The Friends believe "death is the great leveler, imposing democracy on us all". Quaker names like Thankful and Experience abound.

Services are held here regularly. This meeting is associated with those of Falmouth and Sandwich. The three local meetings comprise the Sandwich Monthly Meeting.

JUDAH BAKER MILL

South Yarmouth

On Willow Street, near Bass River, stands this ancient windmill which has ground grain for Cape Codders through the years. This much traveled mill was built in 1791 in South Dennis by Judah Baker. It was later moved by Captain Freeman Crowell to West Dennis. Apparently the population shifted again, for in 1863 Captain Bradick Matthew moved the mill to its present site. Seth Baker operated the mill until 1891.

This Cape Cod antiquity was preserved for posterity by the late Charles Henry Davis, who purchased the mill and kept it in repair. It is located near the site of Davis' House of Seven Chimneys. At Davis' death, the mill and the land on which it stands was willed to the town. Unlike its much traveled neighbor, the Farris Mill, which ended up at Henry Ford's Dearborn Village in Michigan, the Judah Baker Mill remained on Cape Cod for visitors to view.

BAXTER MILL
West Yarmouth

On Route 28 stands an old water grist mill built about 1710 by John and Shubael Baxter. The mill remained in Baxter hands for several generations, grinding corn with water wheel power for the South Sea neighborhood. In 1850 the mill was extensively repaired and converted to turbine power. It was abandoned around the turn of this century after two hundred years of continuous operation. The last miller was appropriately named Dustin Baker and he earned the magnificent sum of 68 cents a day for his work.

In the succeeding years it served as a gift shop and as a lobster stand. Then in 1960, through the efforts of A. Harold Castonguay, local banker and attorney, the mill was completely restored. A special feature is the operation by turbine, the only one like it on Cape Cod. Other mills are operated by windmills or outside water wheels. The mill is now owned by the Town of Yarmouth and is open for visitors in summer. In these days of frozen foods and electric can openers, it is fascinating to see one way our ancestors processed their food.

JOHN F. KENNEDY
MEMORIAL
Hyannis

When the Town of Barnstable wished to erect a memorial to John Fitzgerald Kennedy, 35th President of the United States and Barnstable's most famous summer resident, this dignified memorial was chosen. It was erected at the sea shore overlooking the ocean that the late President loved so well. In front of the curved stone wall is a pool. Visitors began tossing in coins and soon a fund was started that is used for the youth of the town.

Kennedy, who was President from January 20, 1961 to November 22, 1963, was one of nine children. His family rose in three generations from Patrick, an Irish immigrant, to one of the most politically influential in the country. It produced an ambassador (the President's father) and three Senators (the President and his brothers Robert and Edward) as well as a President of the United States.

Barnstable also has an imposing and useful skating rink in Hyannis dedicated to the memory of the President's older brother Joseph Jr., who was killed on a bomber mission during World War II. The whole family has done outstanding work for the retarded.

CHURCH OF
ST. FRANCIS XAVIER
Hyannis

This imposing Roman Catholic church was dedicated in 1904. The parish was organized prior to that in 1902. However Catholics met in Hyannis as early as 1874 in a little church on North Street. Then this larger structure was built on the Hinckley estate on South Street. The small house on the property when purchased was converted into the Rectory.

About the year 1916, the church was remodeled. Four beautiful ionic columns were added to the entrance and the building was lengthened to double the seating capacity.

In recent years this large and active parish became known as the church of the President. John F. Kennedy and his family worshipped here before and during his term in office. It is still attended by Kennedy family members when they are on the Cape.

At Christmas time there is an exceptionally large and beautiful creche in the front yard, erected to commemorate the holy season.

68

JOHN F. KENNEDY HOME
Hyannis

A modest white frame house stands on Irving Avenue surrounded by a high wooden fence. It is within the famous Kennedy Compound which also includes the homes of the late Ambassador Joseph P. Kennedy and the late Senator Robert F. Kennedy.

Originally built by Charles Norris, this house has been occupied by the artist R.E. Pope who was famous for his marine paintings, especially ships under sail. John "Black Jack" Daly, who taught young John Kennedy to sail, also owned the house for a number of years.

Its most famous owner was John F. Kennedy who received here the news of his election to the Presidency of the United States. He served as President from January 20, 1961 until his assassination on November 22, 1963.

This house was deemed too open to suitably protect the President and succeeding summer White Houses were on Squaw Island.

Today the house is owned by Jacqueline Kennedy Onassis and is the scene of family reunions during the summer and at Thanksgiving.

ST. ANDREWS BY-THE-SEA

Hyannisport

The Episcopal Church in Hyannisport began in 1897 with
services held successively in Union Chapel, Hyannis, and in
the old District Schoolhouse which was located near the
present Old Harbor Candle Shop.

Finally, when it was decided to build a chapel, the
Whittemore family offered land on Sunset Hill. The building
was consecrated in 1911 by Bishop William Lawrence.

Services are held each summer Sunday. Any day in the
year, however, a drive to St. Andrews rewards the visitor with a
breath-taking view over the Port, the golf course, Squaw Island
and beyond to the wide sweep of Nantucket Sound.

The Squaw Island view includes the former summer white
house of John F. Kennedy, Senator Edward Kennedy's home
and the summer residence of the Morton Downey family.

ALPHA COTTAGE

Craigville

A choice example of Victorian Gingerbread, this quaint cottage is found on the grounds of the Craigville Conference Center (the old Christian Camp Meeting).

Camp meetings began on Cape Cod in 1819 in Wellfleet under the Methodists. These religious assemblies and Social Outings spread to Truro then in 1828 to Millenium Grove in Eastham.

At first these were tent communities for the summer only. Permanent communities were later established in Yarmouth in 1863 and in Craigville in 1872, where the original camp meeting architecture with its gingerbread trim may still be seen.

Alpha (or First House) is located on Craigville Green near the Tabernacle. An addition to the rear provides space for living modern style, yet keeps the original structure intact. Painters and photographers are drawn to this century-old doll-like structure.

THE TABERNACLE
Craigville

In 1872 a group of ministers from the old Christian denomination were commissioned to find a camp meeting-vacation spot on the east coast. The old record states that when they saw the triangular, water-surrounded land overlooking Nantucket Sound that is now Craigville "they looked no further". The Perry brothers who owned the land laid out a village, sold lots to laymen and churches, and gave land to clergymen and to the group for a church. Known as the Tabernacle, it was situated on the highest piece of land named Christian Hill.

The frame of the Tabernacle was erected that first year and the annual summer services were begun. The building was canvas-topped for eight years and lighted with kerosene lamps. In 1887 a permanent structure was built but the sides were left open.

Today the Christian Camp Meeting and the United Church of Christ operate Craigville as a year round conference center, continuing the summer services which are ecumenical. The Tabernacle now has a redwood chancel, and meeting rooms for conferences. An organ, built the same year as the Tabernacle, was given by Wellesley College in 1960. The antique deacons' benches and the sides that open still remind one of the early days when divines from Yale, Harvard, Bangor, Elon and Defiance thundered their messages across the dunes.

UNION MASONIC CHAPEL
Cotuit

In 1864, when ecumenism was not a familiar word, a great number of Cotuit ship captains met to decide on a house of worship. When it was proposed that Methodists, Baptists and Congregationalists might meet together under one roof, these broad minded world travelers heartily endorsed the idea, having seen people of many races working together overseas. They saw the wisdom of one strong group rather than three struggling ones. These captains promptly subscribed shares worth twenty-five dollars and the building fund of one thousand dollars went over the top that night.

James Childs erected the building at the top of Meetinghouse hill where it tied the two sections of the village together and served as a beacon for homecoming sailors. It was financed through pew rentals.

Later on when the last Baptist had died, the Congregationalists and Methodists built a more modern church in the village. The old Union Chapel still stands, however, and now houses the Masons.

THE OLD INDIAN CHURCH

Mashpee

The oldest church building on Cape Cod was erected on Briant's Neck in Santuit in 1684 by Richard Bourne, noted missionary to the Wampanoag Indians. Lumber was furnished by the English Society for Propagating the Gospel Among the Indians of North America.

In 1717 the church was moved to its present site on Route 28. Among its ministers were the Indian preachers William Apes and Blind Joe Amos who led the Indians' crusade for self-government. Several renovation programs through the years have kept the church intact. An ancient burying ground surrounds the church. Headstones of Chief Big Elk, Deacon Popmunnet and Chief Black Ox are reminiscent of former and present Indian parishioners, members of the oldest Indian Congregation in America.

AVANT HOMESTEAD

Mashpee

This venerable homestead was built in the mid-1700's by a descendant of Richard Bourne, the missionary to the Indians. It is located opposite a herring run reputed to have originally been built by Bourne himself. It is also close to the site of an extensive Indian village. Not far away is Briant's Neck on Santuit Pond where the first Indian services took place.

After changing hands several times through the years, this house was owned for a long period by Mrs. Mabel Avant. The structure is now owned by the Town of Mashpee and is an Indian Museum housing artifacts and displays relating to the Mashpee Tribe. Mashpee is the only Indian town on Cape Cod and is one of two in Massachusetts, the other being at Gay Head on Martha's Vineyard. Both of these local tribes are associated with the Wampanoag Indians who inhabited all of southeastern Massachusetts and part of Rhode Island in Pilgrim times.

CHURCH AND GREEN
Falmouth

The lovely triangular green in the center of town is one of the Cape's loveliest. It is surrounded by 18th century homes and the slender spired Congregational Church (United Church of Christ). The stately parsonage stands beside it.

The church building was erected in 1708 on the green, then later was moved across the street to its present location facing south. The church bell, made by Paul Revere, was presented to the church by Captain Timothy Crocker, a mariner and great landowner. On the bell is the inscription "The living to the church I call, and to the grave I summon all." The date on it is 1796. It is said the leader of the church choir tuned his bass viol to the pitch of this bell.

The beautiful central green is still a center of town life, especially at Christmas when decorations are outstanding. Elijah Swift, the town's founder, planted trees which line the green promising to remove them if they ever became a public nuisance.

FALMOUTH
HISTORICAL SOCIETY
Falmouth

This elaborate, square, yellow house facing the village green was built in 1790 by Dr. Francis Wicks. It has one of the few remaining widows walks on the Cape. Dr. Wicks was a Surgeons Mate in the Revolution. After his release from military duty, he practiced medicine from 1790 to 1798 in this newly built home. Dr. Wicks was noted for being in the forefront of the medical war on smallpox.

The house is now owned by the Falmouth Historical Society and is filled with fascinating exhibits of early days. Each Cape historical society has its own unique emphasis. Falmouth's specialty is recreating Colonial life for fifth grade school children. Appropriately costumed women demonstrate spinning, weaving, cooking, candlemaking and other activities of Colonial days. Visitors may see here displays of ways early Cape Codders lived.

Here also can be seen a picture of Captain Elijah Swift, prominent townsman, who was also a carpenter, lumber magnate, whale ship owner, tree planter and bank founder. The very beautiful garden at the Society house is cared for by the Falmouth Garden Club.

KATHARINE LEE BATES HOME

Falmouth

Between the Green and Route 28 stands a white frame house which was on August 12, 1859 the birthplace of Katharine Lee Bates, American poet and educator. A memorial boulder is in the west corner of the yard. Born here while her father was the minister of the Congregational Church, Miss Bates went on to Wellesley College then later returned there as Professor of English Literature.

Katharine Lee Bates had a varied career as an author, writing thirteen books. These included such varied subjects as religious drama, American Literature, travel and poetry. While on a visit to Pike's Peak one summer, she was inspired to write "America the Beautiful". In it she memorialized her home town of Falmouth, its seacoast, town green and white spired church. There was general appreciation of her poem when it was printed and it was suggested that it be set to music. Miss Bates rejected the tunes that were written for it, finally selecting the music of a hymn written by Samuel A. Ward in 1882.

NOBSKA LIGHT

Woods Hole

The first light at Woods Hole harbor shone in 1828 from atop the keeper's house. Ten years later Captain Edward Carpender, United States Inspector of Lighthouses, visited Nobska. Apparently there was still only minimum equipment, for he recommended that a boat be secured for the lighthouse keeper.

In 1878 the government built a new tall steel lighthouse at Nobska. On top was a fixed white light with a red section to warn vessels of the dangerous shoals. Keeper John Schraff, who took charge of the light in 1925, remarked that on clear days the chimneys of New Bedford could be seen from the top.

Today Nobska Light still stands guardian over the harbor, the only Cape lighthouse with rocks at its base. From it one can see a panoramic view of Martha's Vineyard.

FERRY TO THE ISLANDS
Woods Hole

The ferry *Nantucket* is one of several that carries passengers, freight and cars to the offshore islands of Martha's Vineyard and Nantucket. Leaving regularly from Woods Hole, the boats give tourists an ocean sail and a visit to quaint, historic communities off the beaten track. Island boats also leave in the summer from Hyannis.

Martha's Vineyard is the closest. Verrazanno in 1522 was the first of several explorers to visit here. The original settlers were the Mayhews who befriended the Indians and established several communities. Gay Head Cliffs, gingerbread cottages at Oak bluffs and old homes in Edgartown are a few of the highlights to be enjoyed.

Nantucket, known as the "Little Grey Lady," was visited by the explorer Bartholomew Gosnold in 1602. In 1659 nine proprietors purchased it from the Mayhews. After being attached awhile to New York State, the island was welcomed into Massachusetts. The names Starbuck, Macy and Coffin still predominate. The island is a living museum of architecture. The Jethro Coffin House, the Old Mill and the Whaling Museum are but a few of the many interesting places to visit.

DRAWBRIDGE

Woods Hole

This tiny lift bridge spans the narrow gut under Water Street and is one of the smallest in the country operating on a year round basis. The narrow waterway connects Eel Pond and Woods Hole Harbor.

When a boat wishes to pass through the gut, it blows two long and two short blasts. The bridge attendant flips the traffic light to red and goes outside to close the traffic barrier. The boat which then passes through might belong to one of the scientific organizations based in Woods Hole or it might be one of the many privately owned boats that call Eel Harbor home.

In winter the twenty foot span may lift only two or three times a day. In summer it's another story. The bridge lifts about forty times daily in the congested little main thoroughfare, no doubt frustrating many motorists!

CANDLE HOUSE
Woods Hole

This massive, fortress-like building was erected in 1836 for the manufacture of spermaceti candles. Nine whaling ships called Woods Hole their home port then, and vast quantities of whale oil passed inland from this harbor. The evidences of candle making, which was a side product of the whaling industry, may still be seen in the old flues, hearths and cranes inside the cool, two foot thick walls. Many of the boulders comprising the walls weigh almost a ton. The building was also used for outfitting whaling vessels from its store rooms.

Whaling declined in 1858 when petroleum was discovered and the building became unused. In 1903 the Marine Biological Laboratory took title and has used it ever since for storage of marine life specimens.

The attractive ship mounted on the front of the building is a reminder of the four vessels built here on Bar Neck Wharf: *Incas* 1828, *Bartholomew Gosnold* 1832, *Commodore Morris* 1841 and the Bark *Elijah Swift*.

SACONESSET HOMESTEAD

West Falmouth

Known also as the Ship's Bottom Roof House, this homestead was built in 1678. Thomas Bowerman, a Quaker settler, constructed a house to last, using field stone, mortar, oak timbers and hand sawn wide boards. The graceful 22-inch bended roof is one of the very few bows left on Cape Cod. Nine generations of Giffords have lived here.

Visitors may see in the homestead a welter of furniture, looms, clothes, books and documents assembled through the years. There is a fifteen acre restoration of early farming, featuring horse drawn implements, wagons and tools. One can gaze beyond the grazing sheep, over the marshes to the Bay and turn back time almost three hundred years.

FALMOUTH PLAYHOUSE

Falmouth

In 1949 this lovely playhouse opened with Tallulah Bankhead starring in "Private Lives". Other famous actors who have appeared here include Cedric Hardwick, Sylvia Sidney, Joan Blondell, Paul Lukas, Helen Hayes, Sarah Churchill and Gertrude Lawrence.

Richard Aldrich, who had already made the Cape Playhouse an important summer theater in the country, chose the location for this one and designed the interior. It reflected his experience, imagination and showmanship. The building had been originally used as a night club and a rehabilitation center for veterans.

The Playhouse is located on Coonamesset Pond in a natural woodland setting. It is reflected in the Pond and is suitably landscaped. Inside there is a dining room, bar and place for after dinner entertainment. Luncheon and dinner theater parties are popular here during the summer.

GRAY GABLES RAILROAD STATION
Bourne

On the grounds of the Aptucxet Trading Post stands a tiny railroad station brought here from its original location near the railroad line in 1977. The station was the one used by President Grover Cleveland who summered at his Gray Gables home during his second administration from 1901 to 1904. Cleveland, who was both the 22nd and 24th President, loved to fish and hunt. One of his companions was often apt to be the actor Joseph Jefferson, best remembered for his role as Rip Van Winkle. Jefferson summered at his home the "Crow's Nest" on Buttermilk Bay and fished both ocean and inland waters with the President. No doubt Cleveland found material here for his *Fishing and Hunting Sketches* published in 1906.

When the Cleveland home burned, local people felt it was important to have a tangible reminder of the Cleveland summer White House. The Bourne Historical Society was instrumental in raising funds to move the tiny railroad station to its Aptucxet property and refurbish it. It can be viewed when the grounds are open in summer.

THE APTUCXET
TRADING POST

Bourne

The first business contract in America was signed about six years after Plymouth Plantation was established. In it Governor Bradford and other Pilgrims secured control of trade in furs, sassafras and lumber for six years with renewal rights. The first tangible result was the Trading Post built at Aptucxet in 1627. Two men lived at the Post, trading with the Indians and welcoming Dutch traders. The Dutch anchored off shore and portaged their goods in a 20 mile trip up the Manamet River, overland to the Scusset River and on to new Plymouth.

In 1852 the original foundations were excavated and the above replica was completed in 1930, using the ancient cornerstone. Visitors may step into a two room structure with leaded windows and massive fireplace. The building was constructed and furnished like the original. Herbs are drying and the table is set with Pilgrim bowls and tankards. Glass cases protect the Dutch pottery fragments, spoon pieces and Indian artifacts. A Viking Rune Stone is of interest as is the model of a working salt works down the path near the Pilgrim spring. Actor Joseph Jefferson's windmill studio has been moved here.

RAILROAD BRIDGE
Bourne

The first railroad bridge over the Cape Cod Canal was built in 1910. It was not satisfactory, holding ship traffic up for several days when the tides were too high or the bridge mechanism failed to operate. In 1933 the government authorized the building of three bridges and the widening of the canal. One span was slated to replace the old railroad bridge.

This interesting structure pictured above was the replacement. It is a vertical lift bridge which cost $1,800,000 to build. The 544 foot horizontal span when raised is 135 feet above high water. It is suspended by cables from a tower at each end and is moved down like an elevator to permit the passage of trains then returned to the top position. This bridge took two years to build and the first train crossed in late 1935.

At first many passenger trains passed over this bridge, bringing tourists to the Cape. In recent years however, only a few freight trains thunder across the bridge. It is a majestic sight to see the span lower for a train, then slowly rise again.

BOAT AT CAPE COD CANAL
Bourne

Ships of all sizes, from fishing and Coast Guard boats to huge tankers and liners from the other side of the world, use the Cape Cod Canal to escape the treacherous reefs on the Back Shore of the Cape. The Canal was a dream long before it materialized. Governor William Bradford saw the possibilities when Plymouth Colony traded with the Dutch and he noted the short mile and a half between the Scusset Creek and the Manamet River. In 1676 Samuel Sewall was shown its proposed route. Then during the Revolutionary War George Washington saw the advantages.

August Belmont, the financeer, made the dream come true in the summer of 1914. His private company spent five years and 16 million dollars to build the eight mile long canal.

The Government took over the operation during the First World War then purchased it in 1926. It is maintained by the Army Corps of Engineers.

In the summer time visitors may take sightseeing trips on the Canal from boats berthed at Onset. There are trips available the length of the Canal. These are spectacular by moonlight. During these enjoyable excursions the tourist can glimpse the constant stream of traffic using this waterway.